S.O.S.

S.O.S.

John Townsend

Stanley Thornes (Publishers) Ltd

© John Townsend 1983

All rights reserved. No part of this publication may be reproduced or transmitted in any form or by any means, electronic or mechanical, including photocopy, recording, or any information storage and retrieval system, without permission in writing from the publisher or under licence from the Copyright Licensing Agency Limited. Further details of such licences (for reprographic reproduction) may be obtained from the Copyright Licensing Agency Limited, of 90 Tottenham Court Road, London W1P 9HE.

Originally published in 1989 by Hutchinson Education

Reprinted 1991 by
Stanley Thornes (Publishers) Ltd
Ellenborough House
Wellington Street
CHELTENHAM GL50 1YW
England

96 97 98 99 00 / 10 9 8 7 6 5

British Library Cataloguing in Publication Data

Townsend, John, 1924–
  S.O.S.
  1. English language. Readers. For slow
  learning students
  I. Title
  428.6'2

  ISBN 0 7487 1023 X

Typeset by Input Typesetting Ltd, London
Printed and bound in Great Britain at Martin's The Printers, Berwick.

1

'Help!' This one word has been the last that some have ever cried. It might be yours.

Could you live for long on your own, all by yourself, never seeing another person? Not just for a few days but for weeks on end with just you and no one else in sight. Add to that fear, hunger, pain, a stabbing thirst and a terrible danger. Then think of yourself lost, really lost, with nothing at all to help you. Would you be able to survive then?

Imagine yourself in a tiny raft lost in the middle of a huge sea. Would you be able to keep going? Would you know how to stay alive? The one word you might be calling day after day is that one simple cry . . . 'Help!'

Some people have had to cope with being stranded for months, just drifting on the empty ocean. Some of them have never been heard of again. One or two just made it and reached land before it was too late.

This is a story about someone lost at sea. Some of it is hard to believe. Some of it is too dreadful even to think about. But these events all happened over the last few years. It is a story based on true records of what has really happened.

There were over three miles of dark churning water beneath a flimsy raft – rather like a child's paddling pool with a tent stuck on top. It was an unknown world of nightmares and it was only a matter of time before that leaking raft would sink forever without trace. Time was running out fast.

2

I have always loved sailing. I started when I was about twelve and ever since then I have dreamed of crossing the seas in a small boat. A few years ago I began building my very own boat. When at last she was finished, I just couldn't wait to race her, all on my own, to America. She looked so smooth. I called her *Pippa* after a friend who was slim and sleek – just like my boat.

I went in for a big race where I had to sail hundreds of miles alone across the Atlantic. It would be fantastic to sail across the rough sea all the way to America and then back home again.

All the boats were lined up ready to go. The starting pistol fired and Cornwall was behind us. *Pippa* was soon in the lead, leaping over four metre high waves as the wind grew stronger. But I ran into some bad luck. *Pippa*'s hull cracked and began letting in water. I must have hit some rubbish floating on the sea. Her body was breaking up. I just made it to port where I tried to mend the damage, but by now I was out of the race. I had to pack it all in as it took me a whole month to put *Pippa* right again.

I felt really sad and upset over such a set back – but at least my boat was fit and seaworthy again. The only thing I could do now was to sail on to America and plan for the next race. It wouldn't take long to get there – or so I thought then!

It was mid-winter when I set sail once more. The stars shone brightly in the night sky above the sparkling ocean. The moonlight danced on the silver waves. It was great to be back at sea again in my very own boat. I could never have dreamed what was about to happen. If only I had known that I was about to lose everything, that my life would be torn apart. If only I had known...

I was to be at sea for far longer than I had planned. The whole nightmare was just about to start. I would never be the same again.

3

It would take about one month for me to cross the ocean in *Pippa* – over four thousand miles of empty sea. A gale began to blow and sweep across the white-topped waves. The sky grew dark but *Pippa* plunged on. Gales are common over the Atlantic.

Four metre high waves crashed down all around and spun the boat one way and then another. But *Pippa* could survive any storm. She was built to last. After all, I had made her with my own hands!

As the gale blew, I made sure all my gear was safely tied down. I got ready for bed at about midnight. I was wearing only my tee-shirt and shorts and was looking forward to getting some sleep. It was then that the great whale rose from the deep. The giant monster loomed up from the depths and sprang with a roar. Its huge body smashed *Pippa* right out of the water and into the black pit below a mountain of a wave. I saw the evil shadow of a great green wall of water above me. Then it all happened at once. The huge wave crashed down on top of *Pippa*. I was thrown right over and smashed around inside the cabin. There was a loud roar and an ear-splitting crack. A gush of water poured down on me and for the first time I was aware of what was going to happen.

Pippa was rolling over on her side. She was sinking! My

boat was going down – fast. I just had to get out. That was all I knew. I screamed. Within thirty seconds, half the boat was right under water. Waves kept crashing over me and I couldn't see. I struggled to cut free the life raft. My whole body shook with cold and utter panic. My own dear boat, my pride and joy, was being swallowed whole and being dragged down to her grave. What could I do? I flapped around in panic – that whale could strike again and smash me to pieces.

So what was I going to do now? Who would find me out there in the middle of nowhere? I just had to go back – to go below deck again and rescue as many things as I could before it was too late, before *Pippa* went down for good. There was not much time left. I dived down through the hatch and into the cabin which was now filling up with water. It was pitch black in there and full of churning, angry water. Holding my breath for as long as I could, I tugged for all I was worth at my S.O.S. bag to get it free.

My lungs were bursting and my heart was pounding in my chest. I gasped for air and sucked in salty water. The freezing sea rushed up my nose and stabbed at the back of my throat. I choked and was sick. Then pulling at my sleeping bag, I dragged myself upwards. In that swirling darkness I groped for the hatch and pulled myself out and into the life raft. Cold salt water sloshed all around as I huddled inside the raft with only the bundle of things I had saved. *Pippa* suddenly rolled over and seemed to take her last breath. Then she vanished beneath the waves and disappeared forever.

It was suddenly so quiet. The whale had dived below, the waves closed over the foam and the sea went dark again. I was drenched right through and freezing in that bitter wind – but at least I was still alive! But for how long? It had all happened so quickly. Where was I? Now what?

The nearest land was hundreds of miles away. I knew that much. All I had with me inside my flimsy little raft which danced about on the waves were just the few bits and pieces that I had managed to save. That was all. There weren't even any clothes. All I had on was my sopping wet tee-shirt and shorts. The horror of it all only began to dawn on me slowly. I was alone, totally lost and helpless. It was cold, wet and so dangerous out there. 'But what am I going to do now?' I cried. I tried to work out what I could do but my mind was in such a spin. I tried to think about it calmly. All I could croak was that one little word – 'Help!' But there was no answer. My voice was carried away in the spray.

There was nothing I could do now. It was all up to the wind and the waves from now on. I was in their power.

4

My tiny raft was spun and thrown about in the storm. Great waves crashed down on me, smashing me about inside. It was still dark and I was terrified. I was covered in cuts and bruises. I wouldn't last long in this. I was bound to die out there, nearly five hundred miles from the nearest island. If I drowned, no one would ever know what had happened to me. My family would always be guessing. I would become just another name on a list with the title – 'Missing'.

Water was sloshing in all around me so I had to keep bailing it out with a tin can. The raft was filling up with water and it wouldn't be able to withstand much more of this. It would burst or the thin roof would tear off, yet still the waves thumped and tore at it. They spurted in through the gap at the door, gushing all around and swamping the whole raft. As I was being thrown around like a pea in a drum, I thought again about *Pippa* now over a mile below me and smashed to pieces on the sea bed. Nearly all my food and water had gone down with her. I was on my own now and it looked grim.

My new home was like a tiny tent stuck on a blown-up inner tube. The floor was so thin it heaved and twisted with the swell of the sea. Inside it was very cramped and I couldn't stand up or stretch out. All I had with me was my sleeping bag, a cushion, a plastic box, some sail cloth and the S.O.S. bag which I had saved from *Pippa*. Inside the bag I had some smoke flares to signal to ships, maps, a raft repair kit, a spear gun and fishing line, a first aid kit and a small radio. In fact all the radio could do was send out an S.O.S. signal for up to two hundred miles but the battery could only last for three days at the most.

All I could do was sit there and wait as the sea sloshed all over me. I looked round at my flimsy little tent spinning about on this huge sea. If one wave had a direct hit, I would go under and the raft would be gone. My lips would go blue, my skin would wrinkle and go white and I would sink to the murky depths. My body would be eaten by fish. My bones would sink beneath the sand.

I made up my mind there and then to hang on as long as I could. I would fight to the end for all I was worth. It would be easier to give in and let the sea end it all. But no, I would grit my teeth and battle this out. I would show this sea who was boss. I knew my chances were slim but I told myself that I would survive if it killed me. With my feeble joke spinning in my head and fears of plunging into death at any moment, I drifted into a kind of sleep. It wasn't just my mind that tossed and turned till morning came. My tiny home churned around all night long. The grey light of dawn peeped through the flapping canvas as the gale still raged on. The salty blasts still cut at my freezing flesh like a knife. The waves still spat spray into the wind. The rain still hissed in anger and the sky still roared where it met the sea. But I was still alive!

5

Few people have been able to last for long on their own at sea. I knew my chances were slim and that made me feel worse. What if no ship or plane heard my S.O.S. signal? Would I be doomed to drift till I starved to death?

I knew about some people who had kept alive at sea for a long time before rescue came. The Robertson Family had kept alive with hardly any food or water. I had read their book all about their terror. Then there were the Baileys – a man and wife whose boat had also been sunk by a whale. Their life-raft was just like mine and they were adrift on the Pacific for nearly four months! The thought of this made me lose hope. What about all those people who had been adrift at sea and who had never made it back to tell their story? Many must have died out there and nobody ever heard of them again.

I had never heard of anyone lasting for long on their own. Two people together would be twice as likely to reach land. Two minds can solve problems better than one. Two pairs of eyes are more likely to see a ship. Two lots of muscles are much stronger at rowing than one. On my own I only stood half the chance that these other people had. With this grim thought in my mind, I had to cope with my first panic – the rubber raft was losing air. There was a repair kit in my bag so I tried to patch up the hole in the side of the raft. I also had a small pump so I could keep it blown up but before very long the patch gave way and I was back to square one.

After a while I switched off the S.O.S. signal to save the battery. It was no use. I was hundreds of miles from any ships. This was just empty ocean. The day dragged on and turned into night. Still the wind howled around me, blowing my raft around like a ping-pong ball. The long restless night at last broke into another grey windy day. And so it went on, day after lonely day, night after empty night.

My sleeping bag was always drenched with the salt water and was useless at keeping me warm. My skin broke out in hundreds of boils and sores because of the wet. Blisters bubbled up over my arms and legs, which bled and stung. Cramped up in my tiny raft, I was always rubbing my raw flesh on the salty rubber. It was hard to sleep with such pain.

I began to make notes on a note pad to keep my thoughts and to stop me from going mad. I kept it safe from the sea inside a plastic bag. It wasn't easy to write cramped up in a heaving raft. My very first words were: 'It's all gone. This looks like the start of the end for me. There's nothing left.'

I worked out that I could just about last another fourteen days with the food and water I had with me. But would the raft last that long? I felt so bad about the state I was in that I just wanted to sit there and cry, yet I knew that tears would be a waste of water from my body. I needed every drop I could hang on to!

After a few days the gale at last began to calm down a little. I looked out over the huge wide sea. I was just a tiny speck in the middle of nowhere – a mere drop in the ocean! I worked out that I was drifting along at about ten miles each day. At this rate it would take me weeks to reach a part of the sea where there were likely to be any ships. I worked out that I needed to drift for over twenty days to get near to any shipping lanes – three whole weeks! And of course, if the wind changed, I could be blown back or round and round in circles. Even if there were ships about, would I be seen? After all, I was only a tiny dot dancing on the angry waves. It would be difficult to spot an ocean liner on this huge sea so I knew my chances of ever being picked up were slim.

My mouth was as dry as a bone. My throat felt like sand paper and burned all day. I only had enough water for one mouthful every six hours. It seems absurd that you can die of thirst sitting on a vast ocean full of water. It was so tempting to put my mouth over the side and drink the sea water. But I knew that if I did, I would soon die. Once you start to do that, you can never stop and before long the salt dries you out inside and that is the end. The body must have fresh water, clean and pure.

I did have something for making clean water. It was called a 'solar still' and it worked by using the sun. It was like a balloon which turned salt water into pure water. I had to float it next to the raft. A little sea water would dribble into it and the heat of the sun would turn it into steam. Then a few clean drops of water would drip into a pouch inside.

If the sun was really hot I could get two pints of fresh water each day. But for some reason the solar still was not working very well so it was hit and miss as to whether or not I had a drink some days. If only it would rain! I could save some rain water in tins but it was now so hot and dry every single day. I was in the tropics and the sun was baking hot – a ball of fire burning down on my head.

Suddenly a fin cut through the water in front of me. I had dreaded this moment. I grabbed a paddle to beat it off but as the dark shape swam under the raft, I saw that it wasn't a shark. It was a large fish, something that wouldn't eat me but I could eat him! I grabbed my spear gun. This could mean a meal but my aim was way out and the fish moved too fast. I was so hungry my mouth tried to water at the sight of food! It would probably taste bad but my stomach was crying out for anything. I knew that some of the fish around me were called dorados. They were large blue fish over a metre long. If only I could grab hold of one but I felt so weak as hunger began to eat into me. It was then, with no energy left, that I first saw the shark.

A large grey body nearly three metres long slid silently by. My heart missed a beat – this was a man-eater. I held on to my spear gun but I knew it was no good against a shark. The great fish turned and closed in on the raft, swimming right round me. Its dark glassy eye stared up at me – so near I could almost touch it. My mouth went dry, my arm shook, my skin went cold. I had never been this close to so many teeth before. Then as fast as it had arrived, it went ... gliding silently away into the deep blue water. How many more of them were out there? I would never be able to leave the raft. If I fell out I knew I would be done for. It wasn't just their teeth that worried me. Their rough skins were like sand paper and could rip my raft apart if they rubbed against it.

I sat back and sighed. I thanked God for saving me – this time at least. But was there a God in all of this and would he care about me? I tried to think about such things and have some faith in him. I just hoped he was out there looking after me because I had now been ten days and nights adrift and I couldn't last like this much longer. So I just knelt there in my raft and prayed...

6

The sea was calm and still like a flat slab of blue slate. The sun beat down on my head from a red hot sky. At least I could dry out my sopping wet sleeping bag. My scabs and boils could dry out too. But with no wind, my raft kept dead still and I was moving no nearer to the shipping lanes.

By now real hunger was taking a hold. The cramp inside me was bad enough but my mind kept playing tricks. I would dream of cool fruit juice pouring over clinking ice cubes or of chocolate fudge cake dripping with cream and thick sauce. I could almost smell hamburgers and chips with sizzling onions. Instead, I looked down at all I had left – two rotten apples and some soggy chocolate. I ate them all but they did nothing to stop my hunger or dreams of a tasty meal. If only I could catch a fish!

I knew that if I didn't eat soon my body and mind would stop working. You can only last a few days without the right sorts of food before you become tired and ill. I needed food for energy and vitamins for health.

There were all sorts of fish darting around under the raft. Some were called trigger fish and had little spines on their backs. They were purple with greyish spots and some were nearly half a metre long. I tried to spear one but I was unlucky yet again. I made sure the next fish didn't get away! The spear struck a dorado fish which thrashed about in the water. As I struggled to get hold of it, I had to make sure the tip of the spear missed the raft. If that sharp point burst the rubber I would sink in minutes. I wouldn't be able to repair a large rip. But just as I got the dorado fish to the edge of the raft, it shook free and swam away. Again I went hungry. I was now losing all hope. There was nothing left to eat.

The solar still was not working very well at all. I had to keep patching it up and even then there was not much water inside. As if that was not bad enough, I was not getting any sleep. For some reason the fish kept biting and bumping the bottom of the raft. Perhaps it gave them shade from the burning sun or perhaps they fed off the tiny shell fish that clung onto the rubber underneath. But they always kept out of my reach, as if they knew I wanted to catch them. At least I thought they would be able to warn me if another shark came along. But I was wrong. They stayed just where they were when the shadow passed under us. Suddenly a large set of jaws clamped down on the raft and tugged at the rubber but luckily it didn't rip. I shot the spear into the shark's back but the tip just bounced off the hard skin. The jab made it swim away, only to return that night when I was asleep.

For once I had dozed off but the raft suddenly lifted and rocked as the shark bumped it. I knew that they often nudge things before they attack. It was dark but I found the spear gun and grabbed hold of it as I peered out of the raft. A fin broke the surface with a splash. I jabbed at it with the spear. All went still and silent. I waited and held my breath. I was a sitting target and I knew it. Then, with a sudden hiss, the dark fin cut the surface as the shark smashed into the raft, knocking me right over. I was lucky I fell into the raft and not into the sea! I scrambled back and hit the great fish with the spear and there was a sudden spurt of wild thrashing. All went still again. My heart was pounding and my mouth was dry with fear so I gulped down my water supply in great swigs. It was that sitting and waiting in the stillness that was so frightening. But the shark did not return for its second attack. Soon I stopped shaking and I drifted into a restless sleep.

Next morning I aimed at a trigger fish and I hit it! For the first time I'd caught one! I lifted its flapping body into the raft and struck it on its head. I held my very first fish breakfast! At last I had food – raw and still warm. I sunk my teeth into its salty flesh. At least I knew it was fresh! It was horrible and slippery but I ate every scrap that I could chew. I drank the blood and sucked the eyes to get the vitamins and juices into my body.

The next fish that I caught was a dorado. It was bigger and plumper and tasted much better, rather like tuna fish. I cut some of it into square chunks and strung it up to dry. That way it would last much longer. I threw the scraps and bones as far away from the raft as I could. I knew that even a small amount of blood in the water would bring more sharks.

Although I was thin and weak, that meal made me feel ten times better. For the first time I felt I could keep going for a few more days yet. I slept and dreamed of food.

7

Once again I was smashed out of sleep as the raft smacked down on the water. Sharks! The jaws were locked round one of the pockets on the side of the raft. It was pitch black out there but I just had to hit at the shark's nose. I knew that if you hit back they sometimes leave you alone. There was a wild spray of water and I was knocked over as the great fish thrashed around me. Then all went deathly still and I waited. Nothing. I couldn't stand much more of this. I was like a mouse being teased by a cat – just waiting to pounce. My nerve was about to snap. This was torture.

There were still several hundred miles between me and land. I felt like giving up there and then by just rolling over the side and sinking into the sea. The sharks would do the rest. It was just as I was feeling so upset that I saw something out there in the blackness. It was a light! There was a ship out there and it was only about four miles away! I just couldn't believe it. My luck had changed at last! I dashed around in a mad panic to find my flare gun. With shaking fingers I fired a flare which shot up like a firework to tell them I was in trouble. I jumped up and down and shouted as the bright light lit up the sky and turned the sea orange. 'She's seen me! She must have seen me!'

As the ship came nearer and nearer I threw my things into the bag and got ready to leave my flimsy raft. Home at last! No more sharks and real food! I drank great gulps of water that I had been saving and I laughed out loud. I was ready for a big party. I fired another flare and watched as the ship cut through the waves. The smile dropped from my face. It wasn't stopping! I fired another then another, surely I had been seen. I yelled and waved for all I was worth but still the ship sped on, right past me and into the night. Again I fired but the ship's lights were now only a dot in the distance. I was left with the sound of my groans and the water slapping against the raft. I had used up six flares – all wasted. This couldn't be true!

I switched on my S.O.S. signal. Was it too late? How could the ship have missed me? I screamed and sank to my knees. Dorado fish bit and snapped at me through the bottom of the raft. Apart from them I was on my own again.

I just sat there and watched the sun slowly rise – bright colours melting over the silver sea. It looked so wonderful but it felt like hell itself.

For three weeks now I had been alone – without a single soul to talk to. Three whole weeks! All I had been doing was just sitting there with danger all around and my body getting thinner and weaker every day. Suddenly I heard a voice. I sat up and looked around. What was it saying – who was it? What a fool I was – it was my own voice! I was talking to myself. Was my mind cracking up? The strain was starting to show and how much more could I take of this? By now I felt really low and at my wits' end. I tried to look on the bright side. I was still alive, if I could call this living. I had to do some thinking and make up my mind. Should I give up and watch myself die or should I fight as long as I could? It started to rain. Yes, I would fight! I wasn't done for yet. I caught enough water for a good drink. I felt better already. It was like drinking cool, liquid gold. It gurgled down my parched throat.

Then I saw it – another boat. It was only a small speck but it was getting bigger. It was coming my way. I fired the flare gun. They must see me! It was now so near but I could see no one was on deck keeping watch. 'Hello, help me! S.O.S.!' But however much I screamed, the boat steamed on as if it was blind and deaf. Within minutes it had gone and I was left staring at a puff of smoke in the sky.

Night came, another shark thumped at my side and I pumped hard to keep air inside the raft. The rubber was starting to wear. I didn't know how much longer it would last. One tiny hole would be enough to drag us both under.

Suddenly water gushed down on me, soaked all my things and ripped off my scabs. The sea seemed to be boiling and bubbling. It was another storm. With churning seas and high waves, it was hard to keep a look out for ships. But yes, I spotted another one – was it third time lucky? There was no way this one would see me, it was just too far away. But it did fill me with hope. I was getting nearer to the shipping lanes and the chances of rescue. Was the end in sight? It just had to be.

8

The hours dragged on as I sat hunched up in my bouncing prison. I had to mend my broken spear but at least it helped to pass the time. There was nothing else to do. I tried it out on a really large fish and I actually hit it! The flapping body sprayed blood as I threw it into the raft. It slid about, jumped and twitched for what seemed like ages. It just would not die and I fought with it for a long time before I found my knife to finish it off. My raft was in a real mess and so was I.

All my cuts stung like mad as salt rubbed into them – but they wouldn't heal. They were getting worse all the time as my skin kept splitting. My legs were getting so thin I could hardly stand. I dried strips of fish and ate them every so often with a few gulps of water. But I knew this diet was not good for me. It wasn't enough to keep me going for much longer. The body needs all kinds of different food for energy and strength and I was only eating the same small things day after day. I had already lost so much weight that my bones were showing. I still couldn't get food out of my mind. Instead of biting into a thick juicy steak, I chewed on a fish eye which burst like a grape in my mouth.

I tried to stretch my legs and do yoga to keep my blood flowing. I even scraped off the rust from a tin can to put in my drinking water. My blood needed iron so I gulped it down and hoped for the best.

I drifted from one bit of good luck to one bit of bad. I caught another fish which seemed to fill me with life but then the solar still broke and no more fresh water was being made. I had now been forty days on the raft – almost six weeks alone and starving. My water was drying up and there was only a small bit of fish left. But so far the raft had kept afloat. Now all my time was spent in trying to fix the solar still – just like trying to patch up a torn balloon.

The dorado fish were my friends. I spoke to them and gave them names. They stayed with me all the time and became pets so I even felt sad when I had to kill one. I needed to catch another so I took aim and fired the spear. I hit it but in all the thrashing about, the worst happened. The spear tip ripped a hole in the raft. It tore a gaping hole and the air hissed out in bubbles. Straight away water began sloshing in. I was sinking. This was the moment I had been dreading and it was all my own stupid fault. My legs hung out in the sea. I was being sucked down. I had to do something fast so I grabbed chunks of foam from a cushion and plugged the hole. I tried to sew it and then pump it up again. It held for a while but slowly began to leak again. It would need a lot of pumping every hour but I no longer had the energy. I was too tired to do much more so I slept, only to wake at dawn soggy and cold. My legs were hanging over the side just as a shark slid past. I grabbed my spear and with all the force I had left, I rammed the point straight into its back. The shark shot off into the depths and left me to mend the leaking raft.

I plugged the hole in the rubber again. Now it needed forty

pumps every two hours to keep it afloat. But more and more water had slopped into the raft. The boils all over my body burst open. I was rotting before my own eyes.

I tried to work out where I was and how much longer I would have to drift over this ocean. I worked out that if I kept drifting at that speed, it would take me at least another four weeks to reach land. A whole month! The thought made me feel sick. I'd come to the end of the line. It was all useless and I knew it. Nothing was going right. Everything was against me.

Suddenly, like a gift from heaven, a fish landed smack onto the raft! I couldn't believe my eyes. I couldn't believe my luck! It was a flying fish, the sort that leap from the sea and skim over the waves. I grabbed hold of it and bit into its soft pink flesh. It made a welcome change to the taste of the other fish. Perhaps someone out there was looking after me after all! Yet before long the hunger came right back, but even worse than before. The raft let in yet more water, my open sores bled again and I was still no nearer to land. I was losing the fight. The raft was sagging and so was I. I knew there was little hope left now and my spirits were at their lowest. This was living hell. I just lay there, worn out, weak, in pain and I waited for death. The sky darkened and my faith reached rock bottom. The odds were all stacked against me now. My chances of ever reaching safety were almost nil. 'All right, then,' I shouted at the sea, 'You win. Come and take me!' I had given up.

9

I woke to another magic sunrise full of colour and beauty. A crimson sky stroked a golden sea. After sleep, with the warm sun above me and the raft pumped up again, I felt I was starting to live once more. Then the rain came and I saved the pure clean water in my plastic box. It was so sweet and cool to my throat. I would fight on.

By now I was sure I had passed through the shipping lanes. No one had seen me, no ship had come to save me. My only hope now was to try and make it to land. I worked out that the nearest islands were another three weeks away. Even then I couldn't be sure of hitting them. If I was out by a few miles I would drift right past them and never even know.
It was a worrying thought but I caught another fish and felt a lot better. I ate a feast of fish steak, fish eggs, heart, eyes and fat.

It was my third month alone. At last the showers came. But the water I scooped up from the raft got dirty. I gulped down pints of unclean water full of germs and I made myself very ill. My body was too weak to put up a fight. In the middle of the night I was in terrible pain and in a very bad way. I had poisoned myself.

As I lay there with my head over the side, I really did think this was the end. It took me a long time to get over the sickness.

To make matters worse, my fishing spear broke. That really did worry me. Without fish I would soon die. The tip of the spear had broken off so I had to strap a butter knife on the end. It was a bit clumsy but it was better than nothing and I just about caught a few more fish with it. Yet drink was by now a real problem. In that heat I needed much more water but there was very little left.

Then, as I stared out over the sea, I saw a dark patch on the water. As I got nearer I saw that it was seaweed – a huge stretch of it. I paddled the raft over to it. Some shrimps and crabs crawled around on it so I grabbed a few and popped them into my mouth alive, crunching them between my teeth. Among all the weed there were bottles, cans and miles of rubbish – like one great floating rubbish tip. There were also some birds like sea gulls feeding on it.

These were all signs I had been longing for. They were the first clues I had seen which told me I did share this planet with other humans after all. They were sign posts to what I was looking for. They told me I was getting nearer to land. I must be winning! I was sure I was nearly there.

10

A bird flew low over the water, coming straight at me. Perhaps it was worn out because it tried to perch on my raft for a rest. I shot my hand out and shocked myself – I had grabbed its legs! It beat its wings, pecked at my hand and screamed. I pulled it inside the raft, held its neck and snapped it. Another meal! I plucked and skinned the bird while it was still warm and I ate what little meat there was. I was looking forward to eating another sort of food for a change – but I was unlucky. The chewy meat tasted just like fish!

I spent hour after hour straining my eyes by staring out at sea, just watching for land to appear. But what if I was wrong? I could have got all my working out wrong and missed the islands. I might have to sail the oceans of the world forever. I might have been four hundred miles away from where I thought I was. That could mean another month of drifting. But my thirst burned in my throat like a fire. More than anything I wanted water. It was driving me mad.

Suddenly I saw a jet up in the sky. As fast as I could I switched on the S.O.S. signal. Nothing. The battery was flat – stone dead. Again I put my head in my hands. 'Will this torture never end?' I could see why S.O.S. means 'Save Our Souls'. I was desperate.

More birds and different kinds of fish made me feel sure I

was getting nearer land. I grabbed two more birds which came to the raft for a rest. They were raw and tough but it was food. I saw more ships – but always too far away, too far to see my flares. They were so near yet just too far.

All day my eyes would scan the sea for signs of life and the sky for planes or rain clouds. But the rain seemed to go round me, it always passed me by. I stared, helpless, as tons of pure water fell from the sky just out of my reach. 'Just one sip,' I screamed, 'Just one sip!' But no such luck.

For over seventy days I had been drifting alone and lost. And now was the moment I had always dreaded – all my water had gone, not a drop left. I prayed for the first few rain drops to fall. It was evening before the clouds came over. Then almost without warning the heavens opened. I let the soothing splashes fall on my face and down my naked body. For two hours it poured down, pure and fresh. I caught almost a litre! With the fire in my throat put out for a time, I slept. Pains and sores kept dragging me out of sleep but I kept curled up till morning. If I had known what was about to happen, I wouldn't have been able to sleep at all. If I had known what the next day was to bring, I would not have slept a wink. Tomorrow was the day of my dreams.

11

I rose from sleep and looked out over that same empty blue world. I knew that view so well – just sea and sky, just shades of blue ... But it wasn't! My mouth dropped open in shock. I couldn't believe my eyes. There, as far away as I could see, was a shape – Land!!

I screamed and danced. I drank more water. Could this be real? Was I still dreaming? I had to pinch myself to make sure. I could see the flashing light of a lighthouse. It couldn't be true? After months of seeing nothing but blue, miles and miles of it, I could see green! I would never have thought before that green was the best colour in the world. It was such a wonderful sight for sore eyes!

Just then I heard a faint sound like a hum. It grew louder into a rumble. It was an engine! A motor boat was speeding over the waves towards me. 'Hello! I'm here!' I waved and yelled. Some hands were waving back. It was for real this time, they weren't going straight past! For the ninety ninth time I called out that one word, 'Help!' But this time there came an answer. I was saved!

Three men were talking at me, all at once and in a kind of French. It was so good to hear human voices after all that time, even if I didn't understand what they were saying. 'I've been lost at sea for eleven weeks,' I said.

'Where am I? Have you got any food?'

They said they hadn't any but asked if I wanted to be taken ashore in their boat. All I could say was 'Yes. Please!'

They were fishermen looking for dorado fish. I told them I had plenty to spare all around my raft so I just waited while they caught them all. My pets for the past few hundred miles were gathered up and thrown into their boat. The men couldn't believe their luck. Nor could I! While they caught fish after fish, I sat back and drank my last drop of water – all three litres – I just gulped down that beautiful clear liquid.

At last they dragged me and my raft onto their boat. I could hardly stretch my legs to walk. And so I set off on the final lap of my journey. We were heading for an island. One of the men said to me, 'You are lucky. We only fish here today. We think we see a barrel floating on the water so we think fish might be under it. But it was not a barrel – it was you!'

I couldn't believe the colours I could see on the land. But the smell was terrific! Grass, flowers and trees never smelt so good. It was such a sweet scent – not like the salt, rubber and raw fish of the last eleven weeks. I thought back over that time. I had eaten about a dozen dorado fish, trigger fish, flying fish, three birds and some crabs. A dozen sharks had attacked me.

Ships had passed me by. There had been the cramp, bleeding ulcers, the fear of going mad, those cold wet nights and blistering hot days. There had been terrible storms when the sea tried to swallow me up and then the silent days when the sea was as still as a pond and the whole world seemed empty. There had been that awful hunger and burning thirst. There had been the stress of being so alone and the deep longing to see my family. And now my agony was over.

As we came into shore, people came out to watch. They stood and stared as we floated up the beach. I tried to climb out of the boat and stand on the warm sand but my head was spinning. This was my first step on firm ground for so long and I just fell over. Two men helped me up and took me to a chair. Others went to make phone calls. Crowds came round me and there was plenty of hustle and bustle. I must have looked quite a sight.

But it still didn't really sink in. It was all over. I had won the fight. I thanked God I was safe. Tears filled my eyes and, as I looked out at all those friendly faces on the sand, I saw that they too were crying with joy.

12

I was taken to hospital. All sorts of people came to look at me as if I were some strange creature. But I suppose I was! People kept asking me how I felt and all I could say was 'Hungry!'

They took me upstairs on a stretcher to the ward. I had lost over three stone in weight (forty four pounds or 20kg) but I was told I couldn't eat yet because my stomach had shrunk. Eating could do me harm – but I begged them to let me try! All my ribs were showing through my horrible skin. Somebody gave me a tooth brush and tooth paste. What a strange feeling that was, to taste something clean and minty after all those fish! In fact my teeth weren't at all crusty or black but very clean. They were about the only part of me that were any good.

A nurse took off my smelly tee-shirt and gave me clean dry clothes to wear. I had worn nothing else in all that time. I lay back on the clean dry sheets of the bed. Just imagine it! It was heaven at last. They then gave me drugs to heal my sores and help me sleep. I began to dream and it was wonderful.

When I woke I phoned my family who were hundreds of miles away. They had almost given up hope of ever seeing me again. It was such a joy to talk to them after so long. We were in tears. They then flew out to the island to see me.

They were in for a shock. I couldn't believe my own eyes when I looked in the mirror. I had read about Robinson Crusoe but this was worse! I looked a wreck. My hair was like string, long, straggly and bleached, my eyes had sunk into my head, my brown body was so boney and I'd never had a suntan like it! My legs and arms were like match sticks.

Within twenty four hours the whole world had heard of my story. My picture must have been taken a hundred times. So many people wanted to know all the details. News reporters flocked to the island to hear my story. Television cameras arrived by the car load.

When at last they had all gone and it was quiet again, I looked back over the past months and began to think about it all. I had been lucky to get through all this – yet I was a fighter. It would have been so easy to give in. I knew what it was like to suffer. Never again will I moan about life. We ought to be thankful for all we have. I've learned to count my blessings.

I thought things would be fine now and I would soon pick up strength. But it wasn't quite like that. My body needed time to get better. It looked a mess but I was sure it wouldn't get any worse. I still had a few shocks to come. After two days my legs began to swell up. They puffed up like balloons and I couldn't get any shoes on my feet. It was difficult to sleep, I got cramps and then a bad fever. After all that, my hair started to fall out and it took many months for that to stop.

For eleven weeks I had been short of water, short of rest,

short of food and short of any peace of mind. It was still having an effect on my body. I will always be left with the scars on my skin but who knows how my mind will heal? It takes a long time to get over something like that.

The people on the island were so good to me and I was given everything I needed. After two weeks they said I was fit enough to leave and it was safe for me to go. I was on my way home.

I was able to walk without anyone to help me, down to the shore. I walked over the sand and stepped into a boat again. It bobbed up and down on the waves and I was back on the sea – my other home. But this time it was different. Now it's so good to be alive! Life is such a great gift. I really believe that now and perhaps you can see why!

13

Several people have kept diaries of their frightening sea adventures. Some will never be found. There might even be someone writing one right now, out there ... somewhere. So far, the longest that anyone has survived alone and lost in a raft is 76 days and nights. That was in 1982.

The terror is not just in being so alone but in being so helpless and afraid. No fresh fruit and vegetables in the diet can dull the mind and make the arms and legs stiff or swollen. Without the right vitamins the knees and elbows just won't work. All the fat in the body will be used up and it takes a long time to build up all the energy again. Women tend to have more fat in their bodies than men so they can often last longer in cases like this!

Perhaps this story of survival makes you think about your own life and what the important things in it are. After all, anybody could find themselves calling out for help at some time. One day you might have to cry that one word, 'Help!' It might even be an S.O.S. It could be today. Who knows?

Other Spirals Titles

Stories

Jim Alderson
Crash in the Jungle
The Witch Princess

Jan Carew
Death Comes to the Circus
Footprints in the Sand

Susan Duberley
The Ring

**Keith Fletcher and
Susan Duberley**
Nightmare lake

John Goodwin
Ghost Train
Dead-end Job

Paul Groves
Not that I'm Work-shy

Anita Jackson
The Actor
The Austin Seven
Bennet Manor
Dreams
The Ear
A Game of Life or Death
No Rent to Pay

Paul Jennings
Eye of Evil
Maggot

Margaret Loxton
The Dark Shadow

Patrick Nobes
Ghost Writer

David Orme
The Haunted Asteroids
City of the Roborgs

Kevin Philbin
Summer of the Werewolf

John Townsend
Beware the Morris Minor
Fame and Fortune
SOS
Night Beast

Plays

Jan Carew
Computer Killer
No Entry
Time Loop

John Godfrey
When I Count to Three

Paul Groves
Tell Me Where it Hurts

Barbara Mitchelhill
Punchlines
The Ramsbottoms at Home

John Townsend
Cheer and Groan
Hanging by a Fred
The Lighthouse Keeper's Secret
Making a Splash
Over and Out
Taking the Plunge
Breaking the Ice
Cowboys, Jelly and Custard
Spilling the Beans
Rocking the Boat

David Walke
The Good, the Bad and the Bungle
Package Holiday